QUAKE

QUAKE

THE BIG CANTERBURY EARTHQUAKE OF 2010

PHOTOGRAPHS DAVID WETHEY
TEXT IAN STUART

HarperCollins*Publishers*

HarperCollins*Publishers*

First published in 2010
by HarperCollins*Publishers (New Zealand) Limited*
PO Box 1, Shortland Street, Auckland 1140

Text copyright © Ian Stuart 2010
Photographs copyright © David Wethey 2010

HarperCollins*Publishers*
31 View Road, Glenfield, Auckland 0627, New Zealand
25 Ryde Road, Pymble, Sydney, NSW 2073, Australia
A 53, Sector 57, Noida, UP, India
77–85 Fulham Palace Road, London W6 8JB, United Kingdom
2 Bloor Street East, 20th floor, Toronto, Ontario M4W 1A8, Canada
10 East 53rd Street, New York, NY 10022, USA

National Library of New Zealand Cataloguing-in-Publication Data

Stuart, Ian, 1950-
Quake : the big Canterbury earthquake of 2010 / Ian Stuart ;
photographs by David Wethey.
ISBN 978-1-86950-915-6
1. Earthquakes—New Zealand—Christchurch.
2. Earthquakes—New Zealand—Waimakariri District.
3. Earthquakes—New Zealand—Selwyn District.
I. Wethey, David. II. Title.
993.8304—dc 22

Cover design by Carolyn Lewis
Typesetting by Springfield West

Printed by Printlink, Wellington

FOREWORD

As Mayor of the beautiful Garden City of Christchurch, I found it heart-breaking to see the extensive damage to the city and the surrounding districts caused by the earthquake that hit our region on 4 September 2010.

Most of our city's residents along with those in the neighbouring districts of Waimakariri and Selwyn lost something, ranging from their homes or businesses through to damage to treasured possessions.

Yet in spite of the damage to houses, churches, buildings and basic infrastructure, the miracle is that no one was killed as a direct result of the earthquake.

One of the impressive things to emerge from this terrible act of nature has been the indomitable spirit of the people of Christchurch and surrounding districts. Where would you start to say thank you to the thousands of volunteers who helped those most affected?

That Canterbury spirit fills me with a great feeling of pride to be a New Zealander and to be the Mayor of a city where people can do so much for others in such desperate need when they are facing their own traumas.

The rebuilding of Canterbury will take a long time. The Government is committed to stand beside the people of Canterbury in that rebuilding process. And the support we are receiving from throughout the country is heartwarming and overwhelming.

Thank you.

Bob Parker
Mayor
City of Christchurch

CONTENTS

Darfield earthquake fault trace

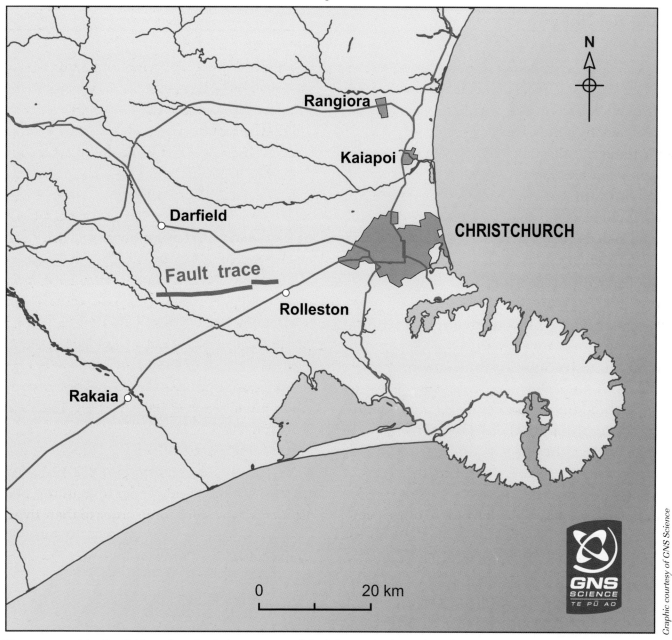

The rupture of the Darfield earthquake fault trace caused the 7.1-magnitude earthquake on 4 September 2010.

PREFACE

Early in the morning on 4 September 2010, the Garden City of Christchurch on the east coast of the South Island of New Zealand was brutally shaken awake by a massive earthquake.

The 7.1-magnitude shake damaged a city which was simply not prepared for such a calamitous act of Mother Nature. That there was no loss of life left many people shaking their heads in disbelief as they surveyed the damage which changed the face of Christchurch forever.

To give a definitive coverage of the earthquake is impossible. Everyone has a story and this is an account of the first few days seen through the lens of one camera.

The response to this natural disaster, by the Christchurch City Council, Civil Defence, the government and the people who lived through this trauma, was nothing short of extraordinary.

It brought out the best in people — friends, neighbours and the nameless and countless good Samaritans.

There were people who climbed onto their neighbours' roofs to make dangerous chimneys safe. There were the strangers who asked simply but with sincerity, 'Are you okay?' There were volunteers who put aside concerns for their own families to help others.

They are the people who make this community of Canterbury a great community. Add to that the support from around the country. It came from all manner of businesses and individuals and it showed New Zealand is a small country and that we are in this together.

It also brought out the worst in people. There were the burglars and looters who saw the opportunity to make the most out of the heartache of others. They got little sympathy.

This book does not attempt to explain why or how it happened. Rather, it is a pictorial record of what happened, so that years from now the people of Canterbury might reflect on how harshly Mother Nature sometimes shows us who is in charge.

It is compiled by veteran New Zealand newsmen, photographer Dave Wethey and journalist Ian Stuart.

Everyone associated with this book has willingly agreed that a percentage of the proceeds will go to the relief fund set up to help the people of Canterbury restore some order to their lives.

Ian Stuart and David Wethey

INTRODUCTION

Saturday, 4 September 2010

An hour or so before the sun rose on a spring day, Christchurch and the surrounding districts peacefully slept.

The bars and clubs had closed, there were a few taxi drivers about the streets for late-night revellers, but most people slumbered on, unaware of how brutally and frighteningly they were about to greet the new day.

At 4.35 a.m. the slumbers came to a terrifying and earth-shattering end.

A huge and destructive earthquake of magnitude 7.1 on the Richter scale began shaking the Garden City and surrounding districts in a way which no one could have predicted. It shook them to their very roots and forever changed the face of the country's second-largest city.

The earthquake, at first reported to be a 7.4 magnitude but later downgraded to 7.1, caused unimaginable damage.

It was later described by Prime Minister John Key as the worst natural disaster in New Zealand's history.

The earthquake left the province shaken, battered and bruised, with a damages bill of billions of dollars.

The repair bill was first put at a staggering $2 billion but within days it doubled to $4 billion and is likely to go higher. Within those first few days, more than 66,000 claims had been lodged with the Earthquake Commission.

But in spite of the damage to an estimated 100,000 homes, to the commercial centre of the city, to roads, footpaths, water, sewage and gas pipes, the area's basic infrastructure, and to the landscape, miraculously no one was killed and only two were seriously hurt. One person succumbed to a heart attack, possibly brought on by the stress.

Had the earthquake hit a few hours earlier or a few hours later when the streets, the cafés, the coffee shops and businesses were doing their normal trade, authorities fear the death toll would have been in the hundreds.

Authorities also believe New Zealand's building codes played a part. Had buildings not been built to survive earthquakes, many would have become death traps. Many of the damaged buildings were built before the Second World War and those brick and masonry buildings tended to be the worst affected, often with bricks cascading onto the roads and footpaths as the unreinforced walls crumbled under the violent shaking.

Badly shaken, confused and scared, the people

of Canterbury looked in shock and amazement at the damage and wondered how they had survived.

The force of the earthquake threw people from their beds, literally. It sent brick walls crashing down onto streets and cars and caused many thousands of chimneys to crash through roofs, often onto beds where, moments earlier, people had been sleeping.

It made the earth ripple and buckle, from Kaiapoi, just north of Christchurch to Darfield in the west and Temuka some distance to the south.

In a heartbeat most of the city lost power, water and sewerage services as the ground buckled and shook with a terrifying violence.

It tore up streets, cracked the concrete slabs on which many homes were built, put cracks through homes otherwise thought to be solid and rendered many old brick homes uninhabitable as the walls cracked and took on a dangerous lean or bowed outwards.

The scale of the disaster took days to sink in.

'I just could not believe it. This is Christchurch. This sort of thing just doesn't happen here,' said one man, echoing the thoughts of many thousands of his friends, his neighbours and people all over Canterbury.

The earthquake epicentre was situated at Darfield, about 40 km west of Christchurch. It was relatively shallow and the aftershocks lasted for weeks.

'The ground,' said one girl, 'shook like jelly.'

For others the sound of smashing, crashing glass in their homes as they lay in bed or dived for cover is a memory which will not quickly fade.

Many, particularly in Kaiapoi, had to come to terms with a natural phenomenon they previously knew nothing of — liquefaction.

Those with some knowledge of earthquakes and geology knew what it meant. When the earth shakes with the violence of a severe earthquake, underground water is forced upward, turning soft and unconsolidated material into a slushy, muddy purée.

Many Christchurch homes were built on relatively soft ground. They shook and rocked, often with liquid coming up almost like a small fountain or clogging the broken streets.

It left a drying and hardening sludge which had to be shovelled up and carted away. It could not be left to run down the stormwater pipes — those that were undamaged — for fear of causing serious blockages.

The shaking cracked many concrete foundation slabs, leaving houses that appeared relatively undamaged but which will now fall to the demolition hammer.

The fate of many homes was quite clear. As they sat twisted and broken on their foundations it was only a matter of time before they got a red sticker indicating they were too damaged and dangerous to live in. A red sticker was not a demolition order but it sealed the fate of many homes and they were demolished because they were too damaged to repair.

It was simply heartbreaking.

One couple moved into their new house on Friday night and celebrated with a glass or two of wine. Hours later it had been damaged beyond repair.

Much of Canterbury's heritage lay in rubble.

The Deans family homestead in Homebush, built more than 154 years ago, and one of the historic icons of Christchurch, looked as if it has been attacked with a wrecking ball. So did the Gunyah Country Lodge in Glenroy, about 45 km west of the city.

The imposing, 101-year-old St John's Church in Hororata, 40 km west of Christchurch, also had gaping holes in its roof.

The main shake was only the start. As the day wore on, aftershocks brought down more buildings as they continued to rock the province, jangling already taut nerves almost to breaking point.

For the first day or two Canterbury focused on the necessities of life. Those whose homes had been damaged or destroyed needed somewhere to live; those still in their homes needed to make sure they were safe and that a chimney or wall was not going to fall on them as the aftershocks continued.

Less than six hours after the earthquake, Christchurch was declared a state of emergency and the centre of the city was closed off. A cordon was established, with Madras, St Asaph, Montreal and Kilmore streets marking the no-go zone. It was too dangerous with glass and bricks still falling. A 7 p.m. to 7 a.m. curfew kept people out of town, mostly for their own safety.

The Civil Defence organization and the Christchurch City Council under Mayor Bob Parker began a detailed assessment of the city and surrounding areas.

What they found shocked them. Of the 160,000 houses in the Waimakariri and Selwyn districts and in Christchurch, an estimated 100,000 were damaged.

Three relief centres were set up — at Burnside High School, Linwood College and the Addington Raceway. They became homes to hundreds of people who had nowhere else to go.

A mayoral relief fund was established and telephones at the Earthquake Commission and insurance companies were ringing nonstop.

The army arrived to help with the clean-up and with the cordons. Prime Minister John Key was a regular visitor. His first visit was on Saturday as the province continued to be shaken by aftershocks.

The fault line deep under the Canterbury Plains which moved with such destructive force on 4 September had lain dormant for 16,000 years. No one knew it was there and there was nothing to suggest it was an active fault until it began its grinding, graunching movement.

Days after the earthquake the exhausted people of Canterbury still lived in fear but many were so emotionally and physically stretched, they began to sleep through that fear, getting the respite they so desperately needed. They slept instead of jumping for the door with every unusual noise or when the wind blew and a window rattled.

The heavy emotional load was taking a toll. After days of repairing damaged roofs and chimneys, one nuggety contractor told his boss he needed a hug. He got an imaginary one and a few gruff but kind words. It was what he needed.

Most of the damaged homes and buildings were insured. About 5000 were not and that sent a powerful message to the rest of the country, said Prime Minister Key.

The earthquake and the aftershocks brought out the best and the worst in people, but mostly the best.

Some who had lost everything looked for others they could help. Those with working kitchens baked, made lunches or meals and handed them out to those who were doing the relief work.

But others saw opportunity. Within a few hours looters were at work, scavenging from damaged homes and buildings. Most were caught and appeared in the courts when they opened a few days later. It was not long before the cowboys arrived in town too, charging up to five times the going rate for taking down a damaged chimney.

Yet in spite of the damage, in spite of the huge rebuilding task Canterbury faced, in spite of the turmoil and trauma and the upheaval to their lives, the people of Canterbury won the respect, the admiration and the support of New Zealand.

They had taken a huge emotional and physical hammering, they had been forced out of their homes, many had lost everything. They struggled, they wept, they often lashed out at loved ones, and they reflected on what had been.

They were battered and beaten but not broken.

As Mayor Bob Parker told the world on a BBC news hour, the psychological scars will take a long time to heal.

'My guts are just churning up here. When will this thing end? It's like living in a maelstrom.'
— *Christchurch Mayor Bob Parker*

'This is Christchurch; it is not meant to happen here.'
— *Tony Stuart, roofing contractor*

A PHOTOGRAPHIC RECORD

A security guard patrols a badly damaged block of shops on the corner of Manchester and Worcester streets in the city centre. Brick buildings in the centre of Christchurch were among the most badly damaged, with many walls ending up on the roads and footpaths.

Once the home of a Mexican restaurant and a jeweller, this block of shops on Manchester Street has now been demolished, finishing off what the early-morning shaking began when the violence of the earthquake scattered bricks for many metres.

ABOVE: A large block of masonry lies in the middle of Manchester Street, which was littered with the debris of broken buildings.

ABOVE RIGHT: The historic Repertory Theatre took a hammering. Most of the facade crumbled onto Kilmore Street. The theatre was known originally as the Radiant Hall after the cost of building it was met by Thomas Edmonds, of Edmonds Sure to Rise baking powder fame. The theatre will be rebuilt with a stronger facade but looking just as it did in 1928 when it was built.

RIGHT: Buildings were damaged from rooftops to the ground floors.

LEFT AND BELOW: After the quake, bricks and masonry continued to fall for hours.

Many buildings became no-go zones because of the danger. Here, police establish a cordon around the collapsed verandah of the House of Travel on Papanui Road, Merivale.

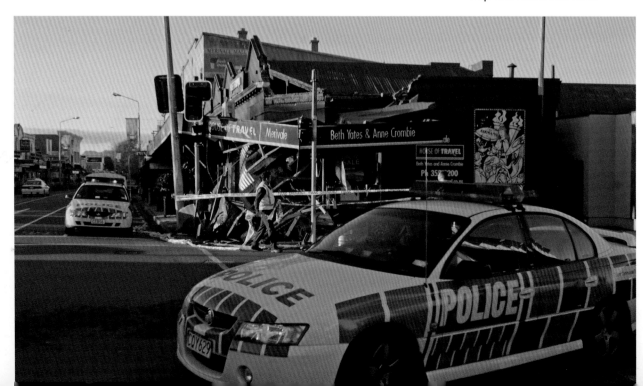

Liquor store owner Frank Pipe lost $40,000 worth of stock in a few minutes when the earthquake struck and the violent shaking sent bottles cascading to the floor. In another big shake four days later, his losses were minimal.

Many brick fences stood little chance as they rocked and swayed in the earthquake and aftershocks. This double-brick fence on the corner of Papanui Road and Knowles Street quickly toppled.

Parked cars were in the direct line of falling bricks. This car was crushed by falling bricks in the suburb of Merivale on the northern outskirts of the central business district.

Chimneys lay on the roofs where they fell, sometimes causing little damage.

Still standing, this chimney waits to smash through the tile roof.

It was all in the way they fell. Some chimneys left their mark on roofs as they toppled. This one in Knowles Street caused serious damage.

Shattered but still standing. This badly damaged chimney in Merivale did not last long after the first big shake.

Only a few hours after the earthquake, a house in Heaton Street is cleaned up. Roofing tiles were no match for heavy bricks.

Worried homeowners, fearing more damage, climbed onto their own roofs and their neighbours' roofs to clean up fallen bricks. Vicki Holland helps out her elderly neighbour in Heaton Street a few hours after being shaken awake.

Brick walls and fences toppled. This wall covers a footpath in Rhodes Street.

The damage to some buildings was obvious at first glance but it also ran deep. This antique shop on Salisbury Street was an early casualty.

The first big shake did not completely destroy the building containing the Asko Design shop and other businesses in Victoria Street, but it was demolished a few days later.

Defying the odds. Some damaged chimneys just hung on. This one in Helmores Lane came down soon after the first shake.

The block of shops on the corner of Armagh and Barbadoes streets spills its rubble onto the street. The street sign went the same way as the building.

Almost an art form. Fragile was the best way to describe some chimneys after the shake.

Safe parking was anything but in Sherborne Street, St Albans. A car sits under the brick rubble from a badly damaged house.

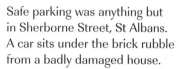

A collapsed roof sits askew on a badly damaged building on Barbadoes Street.

Old character shops in Sydenham, two kilometres from the centre of the city, bore the brunt of the damage.

Building damage on Colombo Street, Sydenham, led to many buildings being roped off.

The sign on Churchills Tavern in Colombo Street, Sydenham, defied the new reality.

A footpath in Sydenham is covered with wreckage from the building.

The traffic light may have been green but no traffic was moving as a small crowd gathers on Colombo Street, Sydenham, to view the damage.

Shaken to pieces. Extreme damage to a building in Colombo Street, Sydenham, where a corner of the building disappeared in a few seconds.

As the earth moved, this timber merchant's shed bulged precariously in Sherborne Street.

Looking after your friends. Marsha Witehira was dragged out of her bed seconds before a pile of bricks landed on her pillow. She examines what is left of her bedroom.

In this block of shops on Cranford Street, the earthquake spelled the end to several businesses.

Beyond repair and awaiting demolition in Cranford Street.

Framed. A picture-framing business on Cranford Street is demolition material after a brick wall collapsed on it.

Taylor Strowger, 10, from Darfield, stands in a deep crack on Highfield Road, 30 km west of Christchurch.

The earthquake epicentre was in Darfield, west of Christchurch, and Highfield Road became a sea of cracks, impassable to traffic.

Grant McLeod, his wife Lorraine and children Shakyla, 7, and Aaron, 11, prepare for their second night in the Linwood College shelter.

Still smiling. Qwinnall Ngaha and her daughter Hilda-Rose, 17 months, are not letting the trauma of the quake get them down as they share a laugh with Red Cross volunteer Lavina Anderson at the Linwood College emergency shelter.

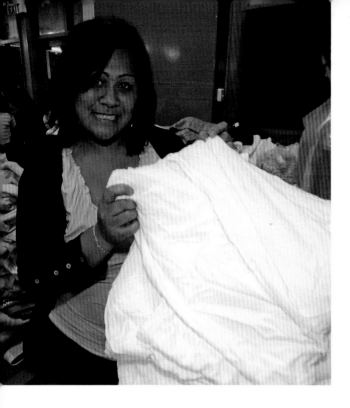

ABOVE LEFT: Volunteer Seta Talaga sorts donated sheets and blankets in the Linwood College hall. It was one of three shelters set up around the city for people made homeless.

ABOVE: Damage to rural Canterbury was widespread and many roads will need completely rebuilding.

LEFT: Brick buildings in Colombo Street are exposed to the elements after walls partially collapsed.

A small room was given a big view for those game enough to use it.

The roof on this house on Bealey Avenue was extensively damaged when a chimney crashed through the tiles.

A log-burner chimney collapsed on a roof in St Albans.

Once a thriving ethnic food and coffee shop on the corner of Salisbury and Madras streets, this building has been demolished.

Part of the pavement on Avonside Drive drops into a sinkhole.

The road surface on Avonside Drive near Woodham Road is repaired but a large fissure remains on the riverbank.

Large cracks in the road like this one in Avonside appeared in many roads around Canterbury.

Bridges over Christchurch's picturesque and much-loved Avon River did not escape the damage, and these two youths took a risk when they crossed a badly damaged footbridge in Avonside.

This fence in Avonside is not missing a paling. Before the earthquake it was intact. After the earthquake it showed how much a section of the fence had stretched.

Cyclists could use some of the damaged roads by avoiding the damage that made them impassable to cars. Like other roads, part of River Road, Avonside, dropped below ground level.

Avonside was hard hit and this type of road damage was common.

Building evaluation team members Michael Nilsson, left, a city council building consent officer, and Dr Andy Buchanan, professor of timber design at the College of Engineering at the University of Canterbury, put a red sticker on a dangerous building in Victoria Street.

Optimistic Christchurch businessman Carl Watkins stands in the wreckage of his hair salon. The building was condemned but it was business as usual in his other two stores.

Charlotte Bishop beside a miniature volcano of river silt forced to the surface of her Avonside property. The house was badly damaged and eight holes gushed slush into her backyard. A week later, Charlotte and partner Tim Baker were married, but not in the church they had originally chosen.

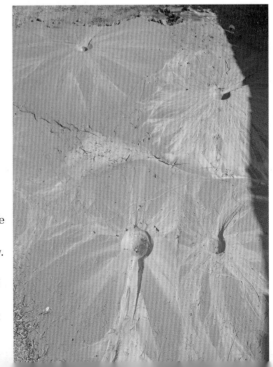

Thousands of these miniature eruptions of slushy silt appeared around Canterbury. They were the result of liquefaction, when water and sediment is squeezed to the surface by violent movement underground.

The demolition of a block of shops is nearly over in Victoria Street close to Bealey Avenue.

Police on duty at cordons watch some of the city's history fall to the demolition machines.

Shabby Chic lives up to its name as the Cranford Street shop falls under a demolition order.

Soldiers helped police on road blocks and city patrols. Helping with the cordon are Private Kauhala Siotame, left, Corporal Junior Maiava and Private Reece Tillson, all from Burnham.

Fish and chips are off the menu. A popular fish and chip shop in Westminster Street, St Albans, is closed for business.

After discovering power lines were still live, digger driver Bill Duncan waits on top of the rubble of a demolition site in St Albans for the power to be turned off.

Three chimneys were wrecked on this inner-city building.

A water tank tilts precariously in the central city.

The clock tower on the Science Alive building in Moorhouse Avenue, formerly the Christchurch Railway Station, stopped the moment the earthquake struck at 4.35 a.m.

Ivan Liddy, 92, remembers the devastation of the Napier earthquake in 1931 and he has now lived through another hugely damaging natural disaster. In his east Christchurch home a meal was delivered by Red Cross volunteer Jo Starkey. The Red Cross was formed after the 1931 Napier disaster.

Suburbs in the city were soon dotted with hundreds of piles of dirt, much of it the product of liquefaction.

For many residents, portable toilets like these in Seabreeze Close, Bexley, were all they could use after sewer lines were broken or the water supply failed.

The rising slush left many once-neat gardens a mess of silt.

Residents of Seabreeze Close in the Christchurch suburb of Bexley pack up and move out. Many homes moved on their foundations and were written off or badly damaged.

In some houses, the slush came inside and caused further damage.

John Fowler's trusty old thermette proved its worth when the earthquake knocked out his power. The 81-year-old made a brew of tea in his garage and used his car lights until daylight as he listened to the drama unfold on his car radio. He admitted he had had the thermette for more than 50 years and it was a little grubby.

No service from this Bexley service station on Pages Road after the ground heaved dramatically out of alignment.

Liquefaction, which forced slush and silt up from below ground, left huge deposits around many houses, like this one in Seabreeze Close, Bexley.

Suddenly the inside became the outside. The interior of the second level of this building in Montreal Street was exposed by a collapsed wall and roof. It has been demolished.

In an ironic twist of fate, these garden award certificates were found when Annette Preen and friends were packing up her house in Seabreeze Close. The house was damaged beyond repair.

In a terrifying moment, Annette Preen had to fight her way out of her front door through the silt. Very little escaped the silt. Her bathroom floor was covered with it when liquefaction forced an invasive mix up through cracks in her concrete floor. Cracks around a living room window show how the house had moved.

The mush from liquefaction spread a long way when it was semi-liquid, but when it dried it became solid and settled everywhere.

Few residents wanted to stay in Seabreeze Close, a relatively new suburb in east Christchurch. Damage was widespread from the shaking and from liquefaction.

Deserted inner-city streets like Worcester Street were closed to the public because of the danger of falling masonry and glass from many damaged buildings. This is the Old Government Building behind Cathedral Square.

Getting the message out to the rest of New Zealand and the world was crucial. Mayor Bob Parker updates journalists at the Civil Defence headquarters.

Principal scientist with GNS Science, Kelvin Berryman, addresses a gathering at the Civil Defence headquarters.

Green stickers meant a building had been through a brief inspection and no obvious structural or safety hazards had been found. Authorities warned house owners to do another check, which could reveal further, hidden damage.

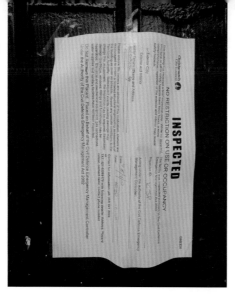

Time out. The exhausted Mayor of Christchurch, Bob Parker, has a rare moment to himself to flick through *The Press* newspaper at the Civil Defence headquarters in the Christchurch Art Gallery.

Fire gutted this massage parlour in Worcester Street in the inner city. Prime Minister John Key and Mayor Bob Parker watched this building burn as they inspected damage to the city.

Without the planning of Civil Defence workers, much of the vital work would have been fragmented and not as effective as it was. A small working group meets at the Civil Defence headquarters in the city.

A sea of faces. Dedicated Civil Defence staff listen to the latest update before they head out to the earthquake devastation for another day of toil.

Danger was always present when the Urban Search and Rescue teams put in temporary supports to this building in Manchester Street. The roof was threatening to collapse at any time without the supports. The temporary repairs allowed occupants to safely retrieve possessions before the building was demolished.

A second-floor office is revealed to the street after a wall collapsed in an inner-city building.

The graveyard of a building is fenced off in the inner city.

The historic Manchester Courts, a seven-storey inner-city brick building with a category 1 heritage listing, may be demolished because of quake damage. In 1906 when it was built, it was the tallest commercial building in the city.

Clearly visible cracks run through some of the architectural features of the Manchester Courts building.

The red flag. Buildings given a red placard were considered unsafe but it was not a demolition order. The red placards meant the buildings needed detailed structural inspection.

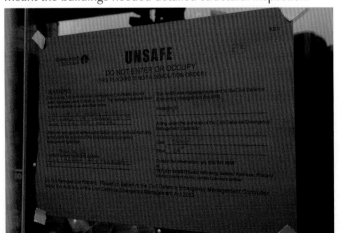

Essence of danger. Before the red, yellow and green placards were put up to indicate if a building was dangerous or safe to enter, spray cans were used to mark buildings.

Keep out. Fences around a damaged building in Manchester Street.

Hereford Street was included in the inner-city cordon.

Fenced and taped off, Manchester Street is almost empty as the city centre is closed down.

Getting the word out. A media crew prepares to film in Manchester Street.

Rubble has been pushed back but the building which housed a restaurant and a jeweller awaits its fate.

ABOVE LEFT: Urban Search and Rescue team members Carl Devereaux and Mannie Hargreaves from Wellington watch their team secure a dangerous building.

ABOVE: Mayor Bob Parker at one of the many media conferences he used to update the country on the earthquake damage and subsequent clean-up.

LEFT: Canterbury's big shake made headlines around the world. Mayor Bob Parker speaks to the media at the Civil Defence temporary headquarters in the Christchurch Art Gallery.

A section of the bell tower of St John's Church at Hororata caused extensive damage when it collapsed through the roof. The Reverend Jenni Carter was asleep in the vicarage across the road and did not hear the bell tower stones crash through the roof and the church organ. She said the church would be restored.

Many of Canterbury's finest historic buildings were damaged beyond repair. The Deans family homestead at Homebush, 56 km west of Christchurch near Darfield, was where part of the movie *The Lion, the Witch and the Wardrobe* was filmed.

Kaiapoi's landmark department store, opened in 1871, has been in the Blackwell family for five generations.

Fractures are clearly visible in this aerial photo of the riverbank at Kaiapoi.

Fissures criss-cross the playing fields and car park of these clubrooms in Kaiapoi.

The foot-bridge crossing the Kaiapoi River partially collapsed during the earthquake.

Some seaside suburb residents initially feared a tsunami after the early-morning earthquake and headed for the hills with their children.

RIGHT AND FACING PAGE:
Seabreeze Close in the suburb of Bexley was particularly hard hit by liquefaction. Properties in many streets were also extensively damaged.

The all-weather hockey field at Porritt Park was hard hit and damage to the surrounding fields is clearly visible from the air.

Two deep cracks show where the earth has moved at Kerrs Reach on the banks of the Avon River, Avonside.

Large fissures follow the line of the riverbank between rowing sheds at Kerrs Reach on the banks of the Avon River.

From the air, the extensive damage to Avonside Drive is clear.

Cranes reach out to aid inspection of multi-storey buildings in High Street in the centre of the city.

One of Christchurch's most visited and photographed landmarks, the Anglican ChristChurch Cathedral in Cathedral Square, was only slightly damaged. It reopened to the public 17 days after the earthquake.

Partially demolished buildings, like this one on the corner of Manchester and Worcester streets, were an all too familiar sight around Christchurch.

The Roman Catholic Cathedral of the Blessed Sacrament, known as the Christchurch Basilica, is likely to be closed to the public for several months for seismic strengthening and restoration.

A crane suspends workmen over the roof of a damaged building in Lichfield Street.

The inner city is shut down as teams work through buildings to assess damage.

Many of Christchurch's older inner-city buildings were cordoned off as a precaution and for more detailed inspections. This view looks towards Manchester, High, Tuam and Lichfield streets.

The changing face of a city. At the corner of Victoria Street and Bealey Avenue, excavators sit where shops once were. Knox Church in the foreground was damaged.

Two of the city's historic icons, the Arts Centre at the top of the photograph and Christ's College, were both damaged. The Arts Centre may need millions spent on repairs but many parts of the centre reopened within a few days. Christ's College reopened nine days after the earthquake.

Damage to Christchurch's new $113 million civic building was estimated at $2.5 million. It was declared safe nearly a fortnight after the earthquake. Mayor Bob Parker said it performed as it was designed to perform and had anyone been inside they would have been safe.

Tarpaulins were suddenly in short supply after they were snapped up to prevent further weather damage.

An aerial view of the new Christchurch Art Gallery, which was used as the Civil Defence headquarters after the earthquake struck.

FAR LEFT: Got a digger? You've got a job. As the list of underground services needing repairs grew, anyone with a digger or excavator could find work.

LEFT: Woody Blakely from Blakely Construction was driving a grader instead of a desk as damage reports continued to mount. This large fissure on the edge of the motorway ramp was repaired by one of his teams.

Repairs began almost immediately. Woody Blakely and his crew repaired the on-ramp to the northern motorway at Chaney's Corner. Mr Blakely said the support he got from suppliers was marvellous.

ABOVE LEFT: Pharmacies in Kaiapoi initially shared premises after the quake before Unichem Fenwick's Pharmacy operated from a caravan in front of their store because the building was unsafe. Running the shuttle service for customers and filling prescriptions were Robert Fenwick, left, Sue Kurokawa, Liz Scott and Sharlene Boniface.

ABOVE: Michelle Cahill cleans up in Fenwick's Pharmacy.

The Blackwell's Department Store in Kaiapoi had considerable structural damage.

The historic Kaiapoi Railway Station, on the banks of the river, tilted alarmingly as cracks opened.

Dave Thompson tensions one of six anchor wires to prevent further damage at the station.

Behind the Kaiapoi Railway Station, surface cracks indicated extensive ground movement.

Paul McKellar from Fahey's Fence Hire barely stopped as demands kept on coming to fence off dangerous buildings. All the company's fencing was used.

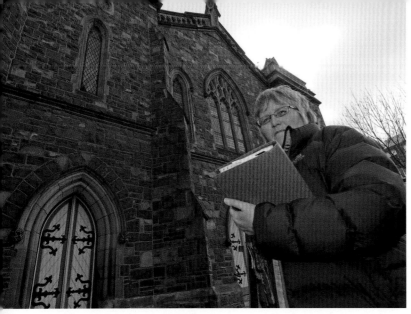

Minister Mary Caygill, outside the Durham Street Methodist Church, needed a new place for her congregation to worship after the historic church, opened in 1864, was severely damaged.

Architect Simon Thomas and structural engineer Dick Sullivan inspect major damage to the Methodist Church in Durham Street.

Students used Facebook to organise people power and earn wide respect in the community as they cleaned up the mess. Warrant Officer Kevin Collins from Timaru briefs the student army at Kaiapoi.

Dirt from liquefaction is cleared from a Kaiapoi yard to be dumped on the street and collected and disposed of later.

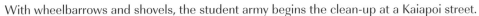

With wheelbarrows and shovels, the student army begins the clean-up at a Kaiapoi street.

Oliver Weller and Caroline Forslund carry furniture from a damaged property.

Harrison Wilson, a Canterbury engineering student, takes another load to the street dump site.

ABOVE: No services escaped the quake. Kirk McDonald replaces a cable at a substation in Kaiapoi after the earthquake caused hundreds of cable breaks.

ABOVE RIGHT: Brian de Lore, owner of Hemingway Fine Wines in Durham Street, feared the worst when the quake struck. He had a display of 37 fine wine glasses in the centre of the store. Not one broke but he lost about 10 dozen bottles of wine.

RIGHT: The international agency Red Cross was quick to respond to the emergency. Stephen Manson, left, Red Cross's South Island emergency management officer, with Christchurch team members Jeremy Martin and Corwin Ruegg, in McBratneys Road during a property check with Gina Aldwin holding Shanae, 18 months.

Frank White shows Christchurch Red Cross team members Jeremy Martin and Corwin Ruegg silt which surfaced on his property in McBratneys Road.

Building control officers with the Matamata Piako District Council Norm Barton, left, and Doug Barton inspect a property in McBratneys Road.

Piles of dirt appeared on suburban streets as residents and helpers began a massive clean-up.

Support from either end of the country. Property inspection teams meeting on an Avonside street include engineer Ross Connon, left, a quality control officer from Auckland, Brendon Wells from the Invercargill Civil Defence welfare team, and Luke Thomson, a building officer, and Steve Tuckey, a building inspector, both from Auckland.

An inspection team — Beth Schollum, left, from Red Cross in Blenheim, Christian Ruegg from the Christchurch Red Cross rescue team and Antony Cook, right, a civil engineer from Christchurch — checks with property owner Emmet Ryan.

Ross Connon, left, a quality control officer from Auckland, and Brendon Wells from the Invercargill Civil Defence welfare team inspect a property as the unsafe chimney is removed.

Red Cross team members Clarence Naude, left, Kazu Miyakawara and Mark Rosny do the paperwork on a badly damaged property on Avonside Drive.

Christchurch geotechnical engineers Shamus Wallace, left, and Mark Foley use a penetrometer to do soil-strength tests on a property in Avonside Drive.

Nothing straight. Many houses, like this one in Avonside Drive, were left with wonky paths and foundations.

Solid footpaths turned into impassable stretches of broken concrete.

Red Cross team members Kazu Miyakawara, left, Mark Roony and Clarence Naude, right, after inspecting Margaret Swift's home.

Tony Marshall from the Department of Building and Housing in Wellington peers at the foundations of a badly damaged house.

Grant 'Yogi' Harkerss, of Smith's Crane and Construction, was in the thick of the work after the earthquake struck. Within hours the company had more than 20 cranes working on damaged city buildings.

Red Cross team members Kazu Miyakawara, left, and Clarence Naude give Edna Moody an update on damage to her Avonside Drive home.

ABOVE LEFT: Dan Coward, left, the Fire Service's Christchurch area commander, in the service's mobile command vehicle outside the Civil Defence headquarters. Senior firefighter Gary Baxter, background, and Station Officer Kevin McCombe, right, staff the communications centre. More than 150 extra staff and four Urban Search and Rescue trucks were brought from as far as Invercargill and Auckland.

ABOVE: In Cathedral Square the clock on the old Post Office building stopped just before 4.30, a few minutes before the earthquake. It is not known if the earthquake stopped the clock.

LEFT: Planning for the first service at the ChristChurch Cathedral after the earthquake are Brian Law, left, director of music, Dean Peter Beck and theologian in residence Lynda Patterson. The service was held outside owing to the possibility of falling masonry in the cathedral.

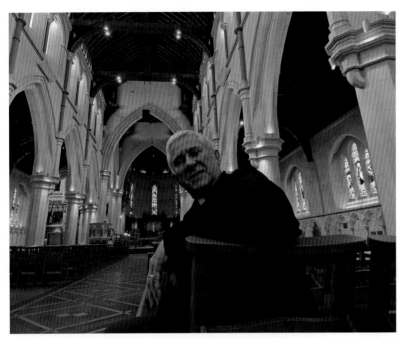

Peter Beck, Dean of the ChristChurch Cathedral, inside the old church. It came through relatively unscathed structurally but some plaster continued to fall during aftershocks.

The red placard on the Valley Inn in Heathcote showed the old hotel was unsafe. The placard later became a demolition order.

The 110-year-old building housing Christchurch's morning newspaper, *The Press*, was damaged and the flagpole and wrought-iron latticework were removed from the top of the building. Staff moved to another building.

The Valley Inn's old safe is gently lowered to the ground on the end of a demolition digger's bucket as the 133-year-old hotel is demolished.

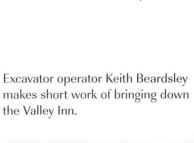

Hohepa Johnson has been a patron of the Valley Inn for 30 years and knocked the top off a beer as a salute to the old pub as it was demolished.

Excavator operator Keith Beardsley makes short work of bringing down the Valley Inn.

Another piece of history falls. The Valley Inn in Heathcote became a pile of rubble.

A small crowd watches sadly as the demolition takes place.

Finished? Yeah right. The 133-year-old Valley Inn in Heathcote Valley is demolished. The Tui sign on the outside wall was salvaged by a demolition worker. Locals had a beer as it crumbled and took home a brick or two as a piece of history. Owner Dean Calvert hopes to rebuild.

Police let no one through the roadblock near the historic Harbourlight Theatre in the port town of Lyttelton. The building, which opened in 1916 as a cinema and live theatre, was saved. Steel girders were put around the outside to stop further damage until permanent repairs could be done. Constable James Bergman keeps watch.

Urban Search and Rescue task force two team members Manu Clarkson, left, Richard Hobbs, Scott Shadbolt and Eric Owsley take a break after inspecting properties in Lyttelton. They are all firefighters from Christchurch.

Bad cracks in the wall of the Harbourlight Theatre in Lyttelton were not enough to lead to its demolition. Locals were upset at the thought of losing the old building and it will be repaired.

The 94-year-old Harbourlight Theatre in Lyttelton was in danger of being demolished but when the Historic Places Trust stepped in, architects came up with ways of saving the old port building.

Workmen are hoisted in a skip past a gaping crack to work on Lyttelton's Empire Hotel.

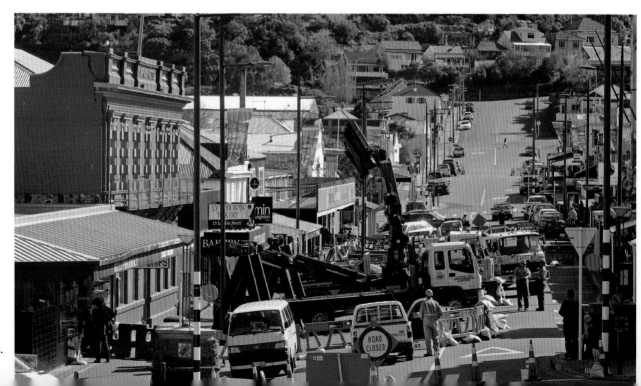

London Street in Lyttelton is congested with vehicles during work to save damaged buildings.

Ever hopeful. The sign was originally put up for a sound building but that was before the earthquake.

Lyttelton's historic Timeball Station escaped major damage. John Le Harivel, from Wellington, inspects stonework rescued during emergency repairs at the station.

Jan Titus, the property manager, under bracing helping secure the Timeball Station.

Paul McGahan, Heritage Destinations southern manager for the New Zealand Historic Places Trust, on the roof of the Timeball Station where two chimneys crashed through two rooms. He said they were 'extremely lucky' the damage was not far worse.

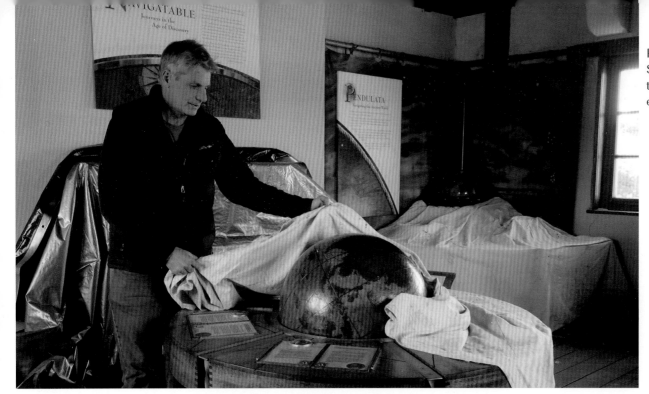

Paul McGahan with the new $150,000 navigational display at the Timeball Station. The display escaped damage.

Fulton Hogan workmen Sam McNaught, left, and Paul Dumbleton fence off an area of collapsed stone wall in Lyttelton.

Many favourite country pubs were damaged, some irreparably. Bad cracks in the Duvauchelle Hotel in Akaroa Harbour made its future uncertain.

The Tai Tapu Hotel was another country hotel closed until a building inspection was done.

Damaged Riccarton shops did not last long once the demolition order was made.

Prime Minister John Key has the backing of Mayor Bob Parker, Civil Defence minister John Carter and Earthquake Recovery minister Gerry Brownlee as he outlines recovery plans for Canterbury.

Mayor Bob Parker and Prime Minister John Key discuss the damage.

Rubble seals off a business on the corner of Gloucester Street and Woodham Road.

After 127 years, The Famous Grouse Hotel in Lincoln fell to a demolition order, after it was declared unsafe and beyond repair. An hour or so after the machines moved in, a pile of rubble was all that was left of the old Lincoln pub.

Kim Bush with children Lachlan, 6, and MacKenzie, 4, at the old Lincoln pub the day it was demolished. Kim worked at the pub when it was known as Bob's, first in the kitchen, then as a barmaid and a bar manager.

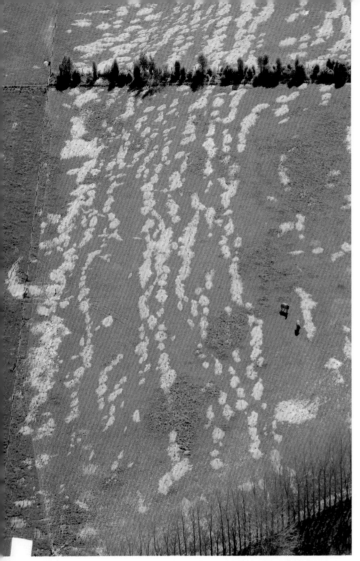

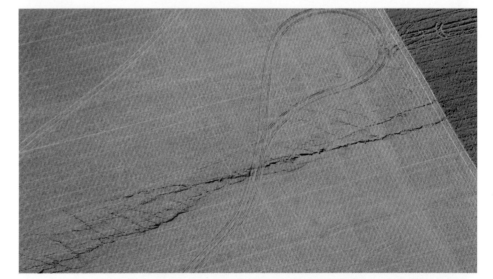

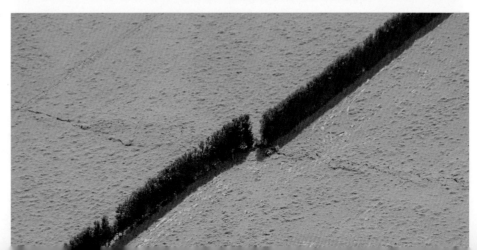

The result of liquefaction covers a paddock with an unusual pattern near Tai Tapu.

ABOVE RIGHT: A Burnham farmer did not lose his sense of humour and burned this message into his paddock.

CENTRE RIGHT: Fault lines stretch across a paddock in rural Canterbury.

RIGHT: From the air, the fault line and the movement of the ground can be clearly seen. This row of shelter trees south of Burnham now has a gap which appeared when the earth moved.

The Anglican Bishop of Christchurch, Victoria Matthews, and the Dean of the Cathedral, Peter Beck, during an open-air service in Cathedral Square.

Eight days after the earthquake, hundreds of people gathered in Cathedral Square for an open-air service. For many it gave them the comfort they needed after the trauma of the devastation.

The Cathedral choir in full voice during the service in Cathedral Square.

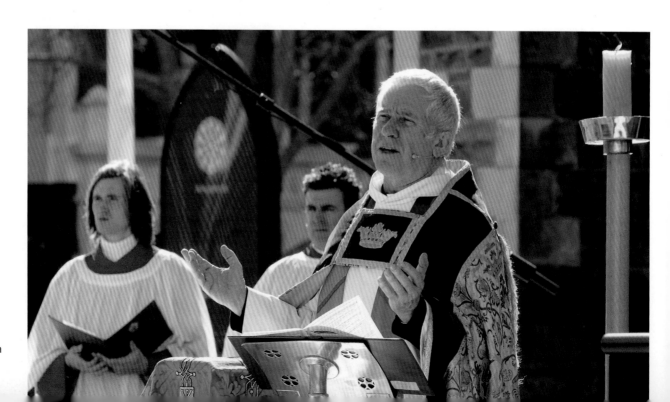

ChristChurch Cathedral Dean Peter Beck leads the service.

Christchurch Mayor Bob Parker and his wife, Jo Nicholls-Parker, sing from the same songsheet during a hymn at the Cathedral Square service. National MP Nicky Wagner is in the blue jacket.

The Bishop of Christchurch, Victoria Matthews, during a service in Cathedral Square.

Mayor Bob Parker and the Bishop of Christchurch, Victoria Matthews, after the open-air service.

A bishop and a wizard. The Bishop of Christchurch, Victoria Matthews, and the city's wizard, Ian Brackenbury Channell, after the service in Cathedral Square.

After the demolition men had finished, this pile of rubble was all that was left of a block of shops in Victoria Street.

Our Lady of Perpetual Help Catholic church in Somme Street, St Albans, was cracked and damaged and expected to be out of action for some time.

Constables Nathan Lean and Patti Brown, from Christchurch, Lance Corporal Gabriel Tuhi and Private Shane Van de Ven, from Linton, with Izaeah Moore, 8, during a patrol in Emmett Street, Shirley.

BELOW LEFT AND RIGHT: Geotech engineers Liam Wotherspoon, left, and Tom Algie, both from the University of Auckland, Russell Green, from Virginia Tech University, USA, and Brady Cox, from the University of Arkansas, conduct tests at the badly damaged St Paul's School in Dallington. The school moved to another site until it could be rebuilt.

The University of Canterbury is a community the size of Ashburton, 80 km south of Christchurch. It has 80 buildings spread over 89 hectares and its emergency response centre in Christchurch was staffed within 30 minutes of the quake. Manager Chris Hawker was in control during the centre's first major incident.

It was a huge job replacing broken glass at the University of Canterbury. Glaziers Joe Taulangovaka and Mark Clements work high on the James Hight library building.

Dr Mark Quigley, a geologist at the University of Canterbury, said the earthquake was very scary but a geologist's dream. He and his partner awoke to find metre-deep fissures in their yard as well as sand volcanoes.

Strewn books in the James Hight library.

In the library at the University of Canterbury, thousands of books lay on the floor after bookshelves toppled.

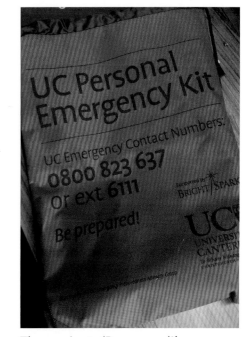

The warning to 'Be prepared!' on a university emergency kit was a stark reminder of how quickly disaster can strike.

Christchurch restaurant Saggio di vino, on the corner of Bealey Avenue and Victoria Street, faces an uncertain future after the earthquake. The restaurant was highly regarded for its innovative approach to food and wine.

Rubble lies in the grounds of St John's Church in Latimer Square near the heart of Christchurch City. The church can no longer be used for weddings and other church events.

The Madras Street Baptist Church, built in 1881, showed severe damage on the masonry, indicating the foundations had been badly cracked by the shaking.

The ornate stonework of St John's Church in Latimer Square crumbled and fell during the earthquake. Because of the damage, the church had to find another place in which to worship.

Roofing contractor Tony Stuart (in white cap) and his son Nick work on one of the scores of chimneys they took down before they fell down. Mr Stuart, a roofing contractor in Christchurch for 25 years, said cowboys arrived soon after the earthquake and charged three or four times the going rate to take down damaged chimneys.

ABOVE: A rare rowi kiwi chick was named Richter after it was born a week after the quake at the Willowbank Wildlife Reserve. Kiwi husbandry manager Corry-Ann Langford feared incubators would fall or the 15 eggs would break. There are only 350 rowi kiwi in the world. Richter will be set free once able to fend off predators.

ABOVE LEFT: The once-straight Telegraph Road, near Darfield, showed the dramatic movement caused by the earthquake.

LEFT: Rural fences also showed how dramatically the ground had moved. This fence on a farm in rural Canterbury was also once in a straight line. The earthquake gave it a decidedly curvy look when it shifted 4.2 metres on Courtney Road.

THE EARTHQUAKE: TIMELINE

Saturday, 4 September

4.35 a.m.: 7.1-magnitude earthquake strikes Christchurch and surrounding districts, epicentre 40 km west of city, near Darfield, depth 10 km. Widespread damage, many houses uninhabitable, many too dangerous to stay inside. Thousands of chimneys topple. Power, water and gas cut. No sewerage.

4.56 a.m.: Aftershocks begin, the first with a magnitude of 5.3.

9.35 a.m.: Civil Defence warning to conserve water and boil drinking water.

10.00 a.m.: State of emergency declared.

12.23 p.m.: Police advise centre of city to be closed because of danger from badly damaged buildings, falling masonry, damaged streets.

2.10 p.m.: Residents of Kaiapoi, north of Christchurch, advised to leave their homes because of damage to town.

5.05 p.m.: Power restored to three-quarters of the city but outlying areas still without power.

7.00 p.m.: Curfew imposed until 7 a.m. Sunday.

8.15 p.m.: Weather warning: strong winds could cause further damage.

Sunday, 5 September

Announcement of Canterbury earthquake appeal to be co-ordinated by Red Cross with promise that every dollar raised would be spent on helping the people of Canterbury.

Monday, 6 September

State of emergency extended until midday, Wednesday, 8 September 2010.

100 water pipes repaired, water restored to 95 per cent of city.

1000 homes still without power.

Tuesday, 7 September

Prime Minister John Key urges people feeling particularly anxious to seek help and commits Government help to rebuild Canterbury.

Government announces weekly wage subsidy of $350 per staff member in small businesses seriously disrupted by the earthquake.

Wednesday, 8 September

Owners told not to demolish heritage-listed buildings without written authorization of the council.

Confusion over buildings with red placards. City Council advises a red placard is not a demolition order, but indicates building is unsafe and should not be entered.

Thursday, 9 September

Boil-water notice lifted.

Residents advised power will be back to all of the city within two days.

Drivers urged to drive slowly in areas of bad damage. Fast-moving vehicles are creating vibrations.

Friday, 10 September

Recreation, sports centres and swimming pools remain closed.

Engineers have repaired 280 damaged water pipes in six days — the equivalent of a year's worth of repairs.

Some cemeteries remain closed as headstones checked for safety. Families advised to check with funeral directors over funeral arrangements.

Sunday, 12 September

More than 200 Canterbury schools prepare to reopen a week after the earthquake after 213 schools closed.

Monday, 13 September

Government announces urgent legislation to help Canterbury recover, saying the building, local government and resource management acts were not designed for the special circumstances Canterbury faces.

Some work can start immediately with consents granted retrospectively. Temporary legislation to expire by 1 April 2012.

Wednesday, 15 September

State of emergency extended until midday Thursday.

Thursday, 16 September

Christchurch City Council advises state of emergency lifted. Mayor Bob Parker says area is moving from a state of emergency to a state of urgency and the area is operating under new emergency laws passed by the Government.

Friday, 17 September

City Council advises services moving back to business as normal and the Emergency Operations Centre is winding down. Resources still stretched and inspection priority given to buildings posing a danger to people or property.

People advised to avoid contact with waterways, rivers and estuaries because they may be contaminated with sewage. This includes fishing, collecting shellfish and whitebaiting.

Residents advised parking wardens back to normal duties by 21 September but that they will get two hours of free parking in council parking buildings until the end of September to encourage city shopping visits.

A BRIEF HISTORY OF NEW ZEALAND EARTHQUAKES

The shakes — year by year

New Zealand has never been without an earthquake for long. Many are hardly felt but others are very destructive, causing much damage to the landscape, towns and cities.

The country's most destructive one occurred in 1931, when the Hawke's Bay town of Napier was rocked by a massive earthquake with a magnitude of 7.8. The epicentre was situated 20 km north of Napier at a depth of 20 km, and the quake caused huge damage to Napier, Hastings and surrounding districts.

New Zealand had never seen anything quite like the Napier earthquake. It virtually flattened two towns, killed hundreds and injured thousands of people, but it also led to the formation of the Red Cross, this country's pre-eminent organisation for dealing with natural disasters.

The Red Cross was one of the first organisations to step in after the Canterbury earthquake and within hours was raising money to help distressed Canterbury people, many of whom were made homeless.

The most significant earthquakes in New Zealand's short history include:

Marlborough, Monday, 16 October 1848

Magnitude 7.8. This was the largest of several earthquakes to hit Marlborough in 1848. Severe damage was caused to houses in Wairau Valley, Cloudy Bay, Wellington and Nelson when the earthquake hit at 2.05 a.m. Aftershocks killed three people.

Wairarapa, Tuesday, 23 January 1855

Magnitude 8.2. At 9.32 p.m. this earthquake was felt across most of New Zealand and caused severe damage in Wellington, Wanganui and Kaikoura. It also triggered landslides, including one which cut off Petone near Wellington. That slip is still visible along the Hutt Road. Up to nine people were killed and five needed hospital treatment. Numerous aftershocks continued to cause damage.

North Canterbury, Saturday, 1 September 1888

Magnitude 7.1. At 4.15 a.m. this was the largest earthquake to have struck the Amuri district of Canterbury, north of Christchurch. It caused extensive ground movement and damage to buildings and was felt on the West Coast towns of Hokitika and Greymouth. As with the latest Canterbury earthquake, there was extensive liquefaction.

Buller (Murchison), Monday, 17 June 1929
Magnitude 7.8. The massive rumbling of the 1929 Buller earthquake was heard as far away as New Plymouth. It killed 15 and injured one but because the area was not heavily populated, damage was limited. The earthquake led to the formation of 38 new lakes of which 21 still exist.

Napier, Hawke's Bay, Tuesday, 3 February 1931
Magnitude 7.8. The Napier earthquake at 10.47 a.m. resulted in 256 fatalities and thousands of injuries. Much of Napier and Hastings was flattened. The cities were damaged not only by the earthquake but also by fires which could not be controlled because firefighters had little or no water pressure. The navy ship HMS *Veronica* was in port when the earthquake hit and immediately sent crew members ashore to help the injured. Without the ship's radios it would have been many more hours before the country learned of the disaster and many more would have died. Like in Canterbury, aftershocks continued to cause damage. The largest — 10 days later — was a magnitude 7.3.

Horoeka (Pahiatua), Monday, 5 March 1934
Magnitude 7.6. The 1934 Horoeka earthquake at 11.46 p.m. shook the lower North Island and was felt as far away as Auckland in the north and Dunedin in the south. One person was injured. It was most severe in the Hawke's Bay and northern Wairarapa, and caused widespread damage from Porangahau to Castlepoint.

Wairarapa, Wednesday, 24 June 1942
Magnitude 7.2. At 11.16 p.m. this earthquake badly shook the lower North Island, causing a lot of damage to local buildings, killing one person and injuring several others. It was centred near Masterton and felt as far away as Auckland, Queenstown and Dunedin. Old and badly built buildings were severely damaged. In Wellington, 20,000 chimneys were damaged.

Wairarapa, Sunday, 2 August 1942
Magnitude 7.0. This earthquake at 12.34 a.m. was nearly as bad as the earthquake five weeks earlier, but was deeper. It still caused a lot of damage to chimneys in Wairarapa and in Wellington. Some had just been repaired from the earlier shake. Another 6.0 magnitude earthquake on 2 December brought down more chimneys in the region.

Inangahua, Friday, 24 May 1968
Magnitude 7.1. At 5.24 a.m. the Inangahua earthquake caused significant damage and was felt over much of the country. It killed two people. It was felt as far south as Otago and over most of the North Island. Inangahua, on the West Coast of the South Island, had a very small population and casualties were therefore light. Houses, roads, bridges and

railway lines were badly damaged. More than 100 km of rail track was replaced. Landslides triggered by the earthquake claimed both lives.

Edgecumbe, Monday, 2 March 1987

Magnitude 6.5. This shallow earthquake injured 25 people when it hit the Bay of Plenty town of Edgecumbe on the east coast of the North Island at 1.42 p.m. Apart from Inangahua in 1968, it was the most severe and damaging earthquake in New Zealand in 45 years. Several towns were badly damaged as chimneys toppled, roads and footpaths cracked and rail tracks were twisted and buckled. It was felt over much of the North Island, including Hamilton, Taupo, Napier and Gisborne.

Gisborne, Thursday, 20 December 2007

Magnitude 6.8. This was an offshore earthquake at 8.55 p.m. which caused buildings in Gisborne to collapse. One victim died of a heart attack and 11 were injured. It was felt from Auckland to Dunedin and on the Chatham Islands to the east of Christchurch. As in Christchurch, it was fortunate no one was killed by falling rubble.

Dusky Sound, Wednesday, 15 July 2009

Magnitude 7.8. At 9.22 p.m. this earthquake in Fiordland at the bottom of the West Coast of the South Island was New Zealand's largest for nearly 80 years. No one died. It compared with the Buller earthquake in 1929 and the Napier earthquake of 1931. It began at a depth of about 30 km and ruptured up and to the south, focusing energy offshore. Energy was released more slowly, reducing the damage.

Canterbury, Saturday, 4 September 2010

Magnitude 7.1. A week after the event it was described as the most expensive natural disaster to hit the country. Initial estimates put the damage at $2 billion but within days it had doubled and was expected to go far higher. The earthquake hit at 4.35 a.m. when most of Christchurch and surrounding districts were asleep. No one died but had it happened when the towns were busy, authorities fear the death toll could have been in the hundreds. During the quake, hundreds of homes were destroyed or damaged beyond repair, the city and district lost scores of heritage buildings, and stately old homes and almost every brick chimney needed repairs or demolishing. Insurance claims were expected to reach well over 100,000 in number.

Figures courtesy of Geonet

THE PHOTOGRAPHER AND THE AUTHOR

DAVE WETHEY — PHOTOGRAPHER

Dave Wethey runs an imaging and photography consultancy business in Christchurch. He comes from a professional career in the newspaper industry, spanning almost three decades, firstly with the *Otago Daily Times* in Dunedin where he became the chief photographer, and then with *The Press* in Christchurch where he worked as a chief photographer, a specialist in digital imaging and as illustrations editor.

He has been involved extensively in the implementation of digital technology and has comprehensive knowledge of digital cameras, applications, systems, digital management and publishing.

He tutors in photography and digital technology at tertiary institutions including the University of Canterbury, CPIT (Christchurch Polytechnic) and Aoraki Polytechnic, and works with businesses, groups and individuals throughout New Zealand and overseas.

He was a judge in this year's Qantas Media Awards.

IAN STUART — AUTHOR

Qantas award-winning journalist Ian Stuart has covered many natural disasters in New Zealand.

In Dunedin in 1979 while working on the morning newspaper the *Otago Daily Times*, he was one of the first journalists at the scene of the Abbotsford Landslide which eventually claimed 69 houses on the outskirts of Dunedin. His book on the landslide became a sought-after pictorial record of the disaster.

He has won Qantas awards for his coverage of the New Zealand troops when they went into East Timor in 1999, and for his interview with Sir Edmund Hillary when Sir Ed dispelled any myth about who was first to reach the top of Mt Everest in 1953, himself or Sherpa Tenzing Norgay.

He has covered fires, floods, earthquakes, murders and mayhem and has interviewed and written about some of most notable, famous and infamous people this country has produced.

He is currently the Auckland bureau chief of the New Zealand Press Association.